PILGRIM,
You Find the Path By Walking

PILGRIM,
You Find the Path By Walking

JEANNE MURRAY WALKER

POEMS

PARACLETE PRESS
Brewster, Massachusetts

2019 First Printing

Pilgrim, You Find the Path by Walking: Poems

Copyright © 2019 by Jeanne Murray Walker

ISBN 978-1-64060-008-9

The Paraclete Press name and logo (dove on cross) are trademarks of
Paraclete Press, Inc.

Library of Congress Cataloging-in-Publication Data
Names: Walker, Jeanne Murray, author.
Title: Pilgrim, you find the path by walking : poems / Jeanne Murray Walker.
Description: Brewster, MA : Paraclete Press, Inc., 2019. | Includes
   bibliographical references.
Identifiers: LCCN 2019002144 | ISBN 9781640600089 (tradepaper)
Subjects: LCSH: Pilgrims and pilgrimages—Poetry. | Sonnets, American. |
   Devotional poetry.
Classification: LCC PS3573.A425336 A6 2019 | DDC 811/.54—dc23
LC record available at https://lccn.loc.gov/2019002144

10 9 8 7 6 5 4 3 2 1

Published by Paraclete Press
Brewster, Massachusetts
www.paracletepress.com

Printed in the United States of America

FOR

Sophia, Adalyn, Lachlan, and Margaret,
who teach me new ways to find the path forward

The moon and sun are travelers through eternity.
Even the years wander on. Whether drifting through life
on a boat or climbing toward old age leading a horse,
each day is a journey, and the journey itself is home.

—MATSUO BASHŌ

Paraclete Poetry Series Editor
Mark S. Burrows

CONTENTS

The Sonnets

I

II

III

IV

PREFACE
My Pilgrimage With The Sonnet

Over the last decade I have felt troubled by the flatness of much contemporary American poetry, my own included. When you get tired of your own voice, as one of my teachers used to say, go back to the old masters. Their strategies will sound innovative. So I reread Shakespeare, Donne, Herbert, and Milton, not to teach them, but in the spirit of an ordinary reader seeking wisdom and pleasure. I was as dazzled by their exuberance and wit as I had been the first time I read them. How different they were from contemporary American verse. What the older poets had in common, of course, was form. All of them wrote sonnets with athletic, pithy, memorable, nuanced iambic pentameter lines. Their efficient, witty language felt catching the way laughter can be catching.

I assigned myself the task of learning to write sonnets. Ten, I figured, would be a good number. Each sonnet only needed fourteen lines of iambic pentameter arranged in a pre-fabricated rhyme scheme. One hundred and forty lines, at most. How hard could that be?

It was hard. But once I caught on to how, writing them became one of the great pleasures of my life. I began to wonder why my experience of writing the sonnet was so sustaining. Why have so many writers used the form in so many languages? In English we have been writing sonnets for five hundred years. But, as I knew, it was Petrarch, an Italian, who first popularized the form as he traveled around Europe in the fourteenth century. I became curious enough about Petrarch to read his sonnets, translated into English of approximately the same period by Thomas Wyatt. I even tried, a couple of times, to read Petrarch in Italian.

By the time I was discovering the sonnet, "free" verse had been around for a century. The poets who had labored to learn the tools of the poetry trade, including rhyme and meter, were long gone. Free verse, itself, had become an orthodoxy taught in most academic programs. It demands practice and skill and occasionally wit, but not the kind found in John Donne's lyrics or Shakespeare's sonnets. In truth, I love many Modernist and some contemporary poems written in free verse. But most of them are not memorable. That is, I literally cannot remember and quote them. Most of them (even the ineffable lines of Wallace Stevens) do not engage my body, either, the way iambic lines do, lines that imitate the beating of a heart. Moreover, the reign of free verse has produced a lot that sails under the flag of poetry but turns out to be prose cut into short lines.

While I was thinking about all this, I was invited to teach poetry writing for a month in Orvieto, a walled hill town in Italy—where the sonnet was invented—in the culture that nurtured the young form. Many mornings that spring, trekking on the town's cobblestone Corso to poetry class, watching new leaves unfold, I'd think of Petrarch, who was born in Arezzo, just a few towns to the north. He probably visited Orvieto.

In Orvieto most people speak only Italian, so my life became a silent retreat. Of course, sometimes I talked. I taught poetry writing (in English) three hours a day. But I didn't have time to stream American news. At the tiny supermarket, Meta, every package, every box spoke a language I didn't know. I didn't know how to ask the clerks to translate. I couldn't even eavesdrop on people chatting to one another in the street. I could barely order dinner in a restaurant. I had stepped out of American hyper-news-time into silence. The town became for me a portal to a different species of time, a new kind of reflection.

In this village, life rhythms seem governed by the seasons. Window boxes blaze with red and purple flowers from April through October. By late November, shop windows are filled with Christmas wreaths and lights. Thursday and Saturday mornings, farmers sell seasonable vegetables and fruit, cheeses, and meat in the Piazza del Popolo. Ancient citizens who grew up here toil up and down the Corso to shop for dinner, to share coffee with friends they went to school with 60 years ago. Trendy young mothers play with toddlers in the kids' park, where they themselves once played.

One Sunday morning we celebrated the christening of the town's newest baby in one of the town's oldest churches. There was something deeply touching about watching the young parents hand their fragile, new baby to the aged priest. And the sonnet is only five hundred years old, I thought. San Giovenale, where the baby was christened, is twice as old as the sonnet. What is new needs what is old.

Late one afternoon that spring, on a whim, I hiked up the Corso to the church, which is nestled in a crook of the town's high stone wall. Dusk was sifting into the valley below as I stepped into the church. My feet grazed the hollows of the wooden threshold worn by hundreds of thousands of pilgrims. I could feel on my shoulders the pressure of ten centuries. The air smelled faintly of plaster dust, of sweet lilies on the altar. I lowered myself to one of the hard, timber pews and closed my eyes. For a long time I sat, held within the pressure of the church's Romanesque balance. Maybe San Giovenale is the least happening place I have ever been. Almost no one visits. I was surrounded by frescos painted when the church was 200 years old, around the time Petrarch was writing his sonnets. Some of them are missing limbs, parts of faces, a whole left side. They gazed down at me. As I prayed, I could almost feel them wearing away. One hour turned into another.

It was either there, in the stillness of San Giovenale, or shortly after that—I honestly don't remember—that I realized the sonnet must surely be infused with a force I hadn't suspected. It seemed, almost, to be alive. We know that in architecture, art, and music certain forms are used repeatedly because they exert unexplained power. For example, the floorplans of many churches (like that of San Giovenale) are shaped like a Latin cross. In music, a diminished seventh incites our passion and by the end of a musical piece we expect discord to resolve itself by returning us to the tonic. We feel safe. So with the sonnet; as we read the last line we feel we are coming home. I began to grasp the fact that, for me, the sonnet had become what I believe it has been for centuries for others: a force of energy so great that the form itself felt sacramental.

Six months later, as orange and yellow leaves fell, I stood with a tour group in front of the remarkable façade of Santa Maria Novella, the vast church across from the train station in Florence. I was listening to our guide talk about the building's architect, Alberti. I caught the phrase "divine proportions." Leon Battista Alberti, the guide told us, inherited and articulated mathematical formulas which he used to structure the façade. These ratios appear in music, too. They were developed in the court of Emperor Frederick II of Sicily. *As was the sonnet*, I remembered. What was going on in that court? When I got back to my hotel room, I spent hours ransacking the Web.

Frederick II, it turns out, was a deeply learned and curious man. He saw to it that Euclid's *Elements* got translated into Latin (from the Arabic translation of Euclid's Greek) and he employed many mathematicians and writers in his court. Among his mathematicians, for example, Leonardo Pisano was thinking up the Fibonacci sequence. Among his writers, Giacomo da Lentini was inventing the sonnet.

Frederick II believed that mathematics and writing are just different ways of interrogating the nature of beauty. Poets in his court in Sicily developed not only the sonnet, but also other mathematical verse forms we still use, like the villanelle and the sestina. And the mathematics of perfect geometry and divine proportion spoken of during those years came to be essential to architects who designed churches like Santa Maria Novella and who renovated San Giovenale.

Six hundred years ago, when these early Italian architects and writers called the proportions of their art "divine," the word "divine" referred to God. They believed God had employed mathematical ratios to create the universe and that those ratios could be discovered and used by painters and architects and writers. The word *divine* has fallen on hard times. It can mean "lovely," as in the sentence, "The ring he gave me is divine!" But the mathematicians and writers in Frederick's court were looking for something very different—a path to God, a way of experiencing transcendence. I was deeply shaken to discover that Frederick II had hurled all his resources into finding "divine proportion," because that's exactly what I experienced as I wrote sonnets, the form that was invented in his court.

My journey with the sonnet has been a pilgrimage. I know that, now, in retrospect. A pilgrimage is a path walked by people who have both a process and a destination in mind. Early Christians went on pilgrimages because they were convinced that by walking the same route as Christians before them, they could experience contact with the original divine revelation that occurred in that time and space.

Walk two hundred miles to a holy place without your cell phone, without takeout, without a map, and you begin to transcend ordinary time and space. Thursday, for example, isn't about taking the dog for a run, driving to work, checking your messages, picking up your child from play school, logging onto Facebook, and making hamburgers. It's about the simple repetition of stepping forward, over and over. You learn how to pace yourself. You enter a rhythm. You become part of the landscape. Time passes slowly. Your mind idles. The hours of a day begin to measure how far you have gone. You imagine reincarnating the arduous and mystical space traveled by early Christian pilgrims.

For me learning to write a sonnet was like that. At the beginning, I didn't know the way, but now I realize I was following a path many writers and readers had walked before me. Learning to make a sonnet requires a writer to submit to a discipline, to recognize a tradition, to practice until she masters a form. As I read the sonnets of other writers, I became aware of writers whose feet had shaped the path I was following: Petrarch, Shakespeare, John Donne, Edna St. Vincent Millay, A. E. Stallings. As the great composer John Tavener testified, a disciplined artistic apprenticeship allows a composer (or poet) to "work with material that is primordial and therefore not [merely] . . . his or her expression, but the tradition working through" her.

And yet, writing a sonnet is not like stamping out yet another fourteen-line artifact the way a Detroit factory stamps out the bumper of a car—as some poets and critics seem to believe it is. The miracle is that the tradition works differently through every writer. John Donne's sonnets are radically different from those of a contemporary poet—even those by Mark Jarman, who took Donne's poems as models for his "Unholy Sonnets." The form of a sonnet satisfies a general pattern—yes—but each sonnet is absolutely and unmistakably itself. As a reader I delight in recognizing the pattern but can never entirely predict how a sonnet will unfold. So, put it this way: to read sonnets is to enter a gallery, to notice how the shapes and colors of great paintings have changed over centuries. It is to appreciate how individual artists have worked within a tradition. It is to savor the ways a form can be adapted. When I read a sonnet now, I am alert to the choices its writer is making within severely limited boundaries. And hard as it may be to believe, those boundaries enliven a writer's awareness of her choices. The demand for a single rhyme can stimulate a profusion of antic possibilities. The obligation to create a volta can electrify a morning. This way of thinking about how art is made is very different from the Romantic "genius" theory, which holds that random (and sometimes untutored) geniuses are struck with inspiration by some inexplicable force they can neither control nor explain, and so they dash off something brilliant. Maybe so. Naïve geniuses sometimes create good work. But a kid who can dash off something brilliant may not be able to score a second time. She needs someone to teach her how to do again what she has once done so well. Most good musicians and poets do not belong to the church of "genius." Most of them have conscientiously learned their craft from the great writers or musicians or painters in their tradition.

I have spent my last several years reveling in the peculiar power of the sonnet, slowly becoming aware that I have been retracing a path many writers before me have traveled. I have discovered the form's uncanny tractability, and I have been riveted by its mystery. A reader who enters a sonnet emotionally and cognitively willing—and who passes through it—can be significantly changed by the journey. As a reader or writer searches, the sonnet slowly reveals itself. For me, at least for now, the sonnet feels charged with transcendent and transformational power.

It is ironic, and perhaps typical of the wisdom of the form, that in the process of writing a hundred sonnets, I have slowly discovered a plausible way of writing free verse again.

But that is a story I don't entirely understand yet. A story for another day.

JEANNE MURRAY WALKER
Merion Station, Pennsylvania

INTRODUCTION
A Map Of The Pilgrimage

The metaphor that governs the sequence of sonnets in this book is simple: to read is to venture with companions on a pilgrimage toward a shared end.

This book's journey begins with the creation. Heavenly bodies burst into darkness. Then comes the earth, people, and, eventually, language, which is "Creation thinking about itself." Human consciousness, expressed in language, feels astonishing, improbable. We speak, we write our names, we realize that the letters on the page spell us, we paint, we arrange sounds in time and space, and our creations convey meaning. Section one of this book displays people performing acts of dumbfounding creation: composing music, arranging colors and shapes on canvas, playing games, inventing slang.

The second section of the book explores less cultural, more personal connections between people—love and anger, forgiveness and resentment, guilt and shame, celebration and quiet friendship. It also pictures our personal and often quirky connections with the creation, our affection for creatures, the mystery of watching and caring for them.

In section three of this book we dare to walk the wild and often solitary path of death and grief. This section records the terrible silence of a dead mother, the refusal to believe it could happen, the loneliness. But the wilderness of grief does not last forever. We venture together toward hope, toward the reversal of death: resurrection.

The last section of the book probes the meaning of silence, investigates the possibility that death may not be the most final silence, that at the core of everything might live a great and true silence that is God. The Scriptures, of course, narrate stories in which characters such as Moses and Elijah hear the voice of God. And in our tradition the Bible itself has often been thought of as God's word. But believers as well as skeptics have also attested to God's silence.

It is silence, finally, that gives meaning to language—out of which language arises and to which language returns. Silence is the white space between poems in this book and even the pause between words. So the journey of these fifty-some sonnets—the pilgrimage of writing and reading them—moves toward the hush of the last page. It's true that silence can appear stifling, baffling, enraging, meaningless. But not all silence is that. Silence can also be elegant and pure, deeply satisfying and primal. And perhaps in our noisy, addled American culture, one way to find God is through silence. After all, "in silence," as Max Picard wrote, "dwells the one uncreated, everlasting Being."

The Sonnets

I

*So there is the city and the river, what people make and
lose and what survives; and then there is the beauty of it.
Here is where we begin.*

—ROBERT CLARK,
Dark Water: Flood and Redemption in the City of Masterpieces

IN THE BEGINNING

It was your hunch, this world. On the heyday
of creation, you called, *Okay, go!* and a ball
of white-hot gasses spun its lonely way
for millions of years, all spill and dangerous fall
until it settled into orbit. And a tough
neighborhood it was, too. Irate Mars,
and sexually explicit Venus, the scruff
of a moody moon, and self-important stars.

And trees. Think of their endless rummage
for light, their photo-what's-it, how their growing
is barely regulated damage. Then birds,
mice, sheep. Soon people, bursting into language.
Creation thinking about itself: our words soaring
like yours through time, dangerous, ordinary words.

SOPHIE LEARNS TO PRINT *SOPHIA*

Remember how the naked soul
comes to language and at once knows
loss and distance and believing?

   —W. S. MERWIN

She twists her fingers around the tall mast
of a pencil, gnaws her tongue, then sighs because
she has to drag the lead uphill and wrestle
it across the paper's wooden flaws—
paper as blank as the field of snow behind
her house. She wants to mark it. But the *S* strays.

Reaching into the grab-bag of her mind,
she aims all her muscles the same way.
She sees her pink hand, blind as a baby sow.
And in her heart, what's that? She hauls it, raking,
scraping, catching on something. Then earth quakes
as she brings out a ring, a sun, a burning *O*
that she sets boldly on the line and makes
it stand by *S*, who waits for it

                tame as a pet snake.

THE VIOLINIST

He owns those strings. His calibrating fingers,
skilled as a magician's, calling with his bow
Beethoven, who comes.

                    Furious, he mutters,
mad-haired, flame-cheeked:

                        and Alps crash—*presto*
con forte.

          This child's music could lure
time from clocks. I swear he could play
till pictures, the sofa, walls would disappear
the way they do sometimes when you pray.

He's young. And yes. I am his charmed mother,
asking music, please keep him from bad weather,
loneliness, ill temper.

                  When he's old, I'm gone,
who'll care for him, I wonder.

                    Then I hear
Beethoven taking the stairs, two at a time,
humming, brilliant,

             always young, still there.

MENDELSSOHN FINDS
THE ST. MATTHEW PASSION

Myth has it that Mendelssohn rediscovered Bach's
lost manuscripts, which had been used to wrap fish.
He did not.

Strolling through Leipzig in early winter snow,
he stops at a fish stall. *Felix*, they call him,
happy, because a skyful of glossy crows
roosts in his mind. He'll coax them from that rim,
later, to perch them on his treble clef,
bass clef.
    To know—imagine!—that he'll compose
what everyone next month, even Hans, the deaf,
will love: the concerto.
      Ah sunlight, good clothes,
and now trout, catfish, and his favorite, herring,
for his dinner. Pointing, he laughs, *These!*

Unwrapping fish that night, he finds Bach's
music, lost a hundred years.
      What yearning
makes this myth more permanent than rock?
Why is it somehow true: he took that walk?

THE MUSIC BEFORE THE MUSIC

When the concertmaster gestures to the oboe,
silence flutters through the massive hall.
Then comes the tuning up. Before that, though—
go back. Before the obedient violin falls
to his A, before the flutes, trombones,
and tuba head like horses in the same direction
to plow and plant one of Beethoven's
great fields. Go back.

                            Hear the nickering run
of a scale, the brash cymbal. A bright lash
of squeaks, the wigged-out chug of a bass viol,
scripscraps of bang and clank, a swirling flash
of flotsam. Go back to unselfconscious style
before style. A grace that's not yet botched—
before they know that they're being heard or watched.

REMBRANDT: LATE SELF PORTRAIT

His face gropes up from deepest dark—a warty
trout from heavy water. Unforgiving light
washes across the bulbous nose, the portly
cheeks, black eyes.
               Who's this? And what night
has he emerged from
                    confused by his own paint?
The sludge-colored mud the painter's thumb
smeared on, as if Rembrandt knew Rembrandt
was breaking down.
              He peers, lost in numb
candor, stripped, unable to go on.

Here in the museum I almost call, *More light!*
and step toward a guard.
               But breaking through—
a hitch of caught breath—a shift, a motion
across the canvas.
            Last sun rips through night
as if the blur of his burly hand had reached for blue.

PHILADEPHIA MUSEUM: LEARNING TO SEE

Then turning the gallery corner you see a
splendid life-size thigh, how it's tapering
to a calf and pointed toe. The shy Degas
ballerina's pulling light on like a stocking.

The ornate gold frame says, *Look at this.*
You've come alone, so why not stay, go down
to the very root of light, practice patience?
Sinking in, you linger all afternoon.

On the bus back home you see your city better.
The sun you'd barely noticed strikes a blaze
through the wheezy door. You love the glitter
of dazzled passengers. You see and praise
legs, bare, scarred, tanned. You praise your own
tibia, small miracle, that sturdy leg to stand on.

SONG OF THE STREET

Play is the exultation of the possible.
—MARTIN BUBER

Praise the babble that rises to my ears
like morning song, the fragrant bling that floats
around me as I amble to my car
in the Big Apple, slang so young it gloats
and wants to slap me five as I breeze by.
Nonstandard diction, discombobulated
syntax. Improv. The shy-wild joy cry
of the young who love their bodies, the elated
cries of hopscotch, double-dutch, stick ball—
English roaring, shattering cliché,
sprung from the school room. I wave and call
to them as English stretches, bounds into a day
of crazy climbing sun.

              This moment you're all quirk
and shine and possibility, New York.

ROCK

Bad rock band, you bend your boomerang
around my ear,
        you nail me.
                I admit it.

Your voice, *baby, baby,* skids and clangs
as if the ripping devil swiveled it,
himself, from primal hell.
               That pleading,
feral, skidding caterwaul!
                  Oh, don't you
just anger up a whole town of needing
voices in one body—from *wahoo*
to *Wittgenstein?*
               Not one ping you jive on
is squelched.
            All holler, hootenanny, flexing
to the glory of a shriek.
                 Stay!
                  Live on
as long as Bach.
           Croon us through perplexing
silences of midnight. Rock us, bless
us. Be tenacious. Blast us.

THE PATH FORWARD

Proper artificing is like a song made solid.
It is an act of creation.

—FEDERICO BADIA, shoemaker in Orvieto, Italy

For coming this far, thank you. Let's stop
before the wind turns cold, put on vests,
lay down our fear of silence.
                                        There's no map,
but I know the cobbler, know his shoes will last;
they almost know the way: a step forward,
another, then another, till you feel the hum
of peace, borne on the alphabet, these words
the path forward, also, our brief home.

Think of him stitching leather, making solid
song as we dissolve into the unknown
crags before us. Clouds wrinkle the forehead
of bright morning. Time past and time flown
become time present and everything we care
for waits far ahead, on the other side of fear.

II

Sometimes an abyss opens between Tuesday and Wednesday;

twenty-six years could pass in a moment.

Time is not a straight line. It's more of a labyrinth,

and if you press close to the wall at the right place you can hear

the hurrying steps and the voices,

you can hear yourself walking past on the other side.

—TOMAS TRANSTROMER,
from "Answers to Letters"

FOREBODING

The twelve-point buck has finished our azalea
and browses, let's say, in some dark meadow
south of us, lifting his bright candelabra
to the moon. Far off, the wavering tremolo
of coyotes, the low and endless snapping
crickets. Field mice, fearing the long fast
of winter, gather seeds. Black crows mapping
an exit. They're all gone, last of the last,
quarreling about the route.

                  Only we stay,
who can't migrate, we who hear the scratch
and fall of leaves, more anxious every day
as darkness lengthens. Earthworms stop and lie
like crooked nails beneath brown thatch.
Last night, a mouse with red alcoholic eyes.

BREAKING THE BLUE BOWL

I am the tiny, irate, scolding person
standing in the dome of my own skull,
she shakes her head, arms crossed, again
disappointed: I'm clumsy, struggling, dull.

Then there's the shattered wine glass,
an afternoon misspent, a dinner gobbled,
rank laundry, unpaid bills, uncut grass,
and, I suspect, one lovely friendship bobbled.

And yet, I'm here. Alive.
                        These yellow swiveling
leaves, this carnival of wind, make me recall
I'd love my neighbor if I loved myself
better.
        The sky's a million geese unraveling
in blue forgiveness. Love the tattered fall.
Forgive yourself.

So what if a bowl slid off a shelf?

THE KNOCK ON YOUR DOOR
DISGUISED AS A SONNET

I've stood by Lake Miltona, watching water,
bored by years of its own angry nature,
finally decide it could reflect the sky,
mirroring blackbirds as they learned to fly.

This is a sky, books tell us, *that's a lake*.
But things fall into one another's arms
to find out who they are. Take a pine and take
the wind, for instance. They can transform
each other, just as water wears down stones.
We shape one another. No man's an island,
Darling. Every stone is—yes—a broken stone.

When I stormed to my room and slammed the door,
I made two rooms—you helpless there, sealed in.
If I knock on the wall, will you answer?

BAKER

The bus releases you beside the bakery
at 5 AM. His light's on. You can smell
the secret life of bread—its russet brawny
shoulders rising in the pan, yeast swelling,
yearning toward croissants, pretzels, braided
curls of challah.

You give the baker money,
he gives you a loaf. Neither of you can say
the mystery you share like lovers. You shyly
nod and bear your loneliness to work
in helpless hands. Whatever it is, you can
not explain the one thing that matters.

You break
his bread at noon and fling it toward frozen
ducks on the millpond and you awaken
from what you've been.

You want to be bread broken.

SO YOU'RE LOSING YOUR MEMORY?

It's gone—your stab of joy at meeting him,
his careless wave and sundrenched face, the sky's
ephemeral clouds, your double reckless skimming
toward each other. Lost, the wild leaves, flying.

And lost the flutter of your newborn's feet,
sweet moth against your arm.
                              You're gone from lofts,
absent from your lost houses, blank in moonlight.
Your wraith fishes for walleyes as you drift
beside your phantom father.
                              Vanished, vanishing!
Dark space where books are missing from the shelf.
In the attic of your skull, you can feel erasing
The Pledge, times tables.
                              And your bruising
mistakes gone too.
                              You can live with yourself
and heal, and your voice grows less accusing.

SELF-EXAMINATION

And then we're each alone—what women do
in secret, slipping fingers under bras or
nightgowns on wild, moon-driven nights to
true the circle of their breasts, explore
below desire, beneath arousal, and beyond
the sweet milk-happiness of feeding children
to find the nuclear godawful contraband
our bodies might be hiding—the refrain—
cancer, danger—singing in our minds.

Like when at Lent I slide into a pew to pray—
alert and combing through my week to find
what might destroy me, to send it away—

both lawyer and accused, finding what's faulty:
the hands that judge, even, maybe, guilty.

TO THE CARDINAL WATCHING
ME SHOWER
—a sonnet with rhymes on its first words

All right, red bird, buttinski, Peeping Tom.
I'm not embarrassed you caught me naked—
your headlights through my window. I feel you drill
the spot between my breasts as I dry off
after my shower. I rather *like* my aging body.

You're not the songbird of my dreams, anyway.
Hereafter, if you let my sags and wrinkles
blear up your love, or if you fly off to sing at
Someone New's bird feeder, then I swear I'll
glue your pages in my bird book together and
entomb you.
                    Or wait.
                              Why not come back tomorrow?
I might change my mind. You could argue:
you mate for life. Your song is sweet and free.
Say this: how well you wear light on your bright fierce body.

FINCH

Valentine's day on the East Coast. Flakes
hum like moths in our hemlock; the Superfresh
buzzes when I dash in for milk and cake.
Strangers laughing, swapping recipes in the fish
aisle. How dear we are to one another,
how shy. Small squirrels of terror leap branch
to branch. At earth's center, the massive cedar
shudders, holds.

               At home, we spot a finch
perching in our red cedar. She barely
holds her own against the threatening clinch
of dark. Our pitch is tuned so squarely
to the middle *C* called hope, we sit and watch
till midnight while she bravely recreates
herself from snow and fear and love of being watched.

THE CREATION

was going well. A perfect, rosy sow,
a finch, an elephant. Then a giraffe
at the last minute, sprang up like *Wow,*
an exclamation point on legs. A gaffe.
Or maybe not.
                    Her fringy eyelashes,
her voice, a bleat soft as a low laugh,
a yard-long black tongue to lick and catch
leaves from the sky. She nuzzles her newborn calf,
still wet, eyes shut, legs splayed and sliding,
the two of them improbable sweet chaff
of the imagination, hang-gliding
off the cliff of reason.
                    Oh giraffes,
gather around, bend down your horns. Remind me,
when all seems dark and sane, of mystery.

AFTER THE BUTTERFLY COMPLETES THE FIRST LEG OF HER THOUSAND-MILE MIGRATION

When the Monarch can finally trust herself
to scan the ground, she sees vast water down
there, a spinning galaxy, whirling shelf
on whirling shelf, the tons of pouring ocean.
Just one island.

            She plummets down to calm
on dune grass, her stomach filled with a bright mob
of eggs, her wings a brilliant stab at finding them
(please God) someplace to hatch, her brain a-throb
with gaudy hope. But oh, the sky's an orchestra
of wind against her—and the ocean's outraged
screams—

            If she could, she'd say—clinging—
I'm tired, God. You watch the universe an extra
hour. As she sleeps, the sun, stuck in the ribcage
of a bare oak, begins to rave *Spring, spring!*

POINSETTIA

The scarlet petals were floppy as felt hats
by March, and falling into piles across the rug,
so I cut the plastic pot to free its roots
and laid it by the compost in the mud.

Busy that spring, I didn't notice how
it waited out the months, night after night
in wind, in grueling rain and a late snow,
inclining from the compost into light,
its new leaves firming, blossomless and thick,
like a novitiate of a strange order.
As mornings warmed, it grew strong and quick
to shade the lost plants I'd abandoned there,
finally ringing red, like church bells, on the hour.
And who knows now which twig will next flower?

III

There is a dove in heaven, we know, that descends when the skies open, sometimes in fire. But perhaps there is also a hawk in heaven that swoops down on us with the gift of death to deliver us from our used-up past, the past we have neither the courage nor the imagination to walk away from.

—Virginia Stem Owens,
Wind River Winter

WHILE HIKING IN FALL WITHOUT PEN AND PAPER, I MAKE MENTAL NOTES

What if I forget the blackbird crying *die-*
we die-we die-we die as I trudge under
the oaks?
        Remember, I tell myself: the cry
that shapes the crier: the small fierce soldier
with scarlet epaulets, who fixes me
in his domineering eye from a low branch.

Remember how his cry cries me. How my feet
are shaped by the forest floor. Recall the crunch
of dried weeds. Don't forget the warmth of sun
glinting through oaks.
        In the copper leaves
that shine in sun like pennies I lie down
and etch my body's outline, hoping to save
it—a lost leaf-angel stirring dirt, mold, grit—
changing the planet permanently
                for a minute.

DEATH BE NOT PROUD

I startle awake to roaring wind, the pine
seething in ice and then recall my mother,
dying in Texas. I'll fly to her again
tomorrow with nothing in my hands to save her.

Through the window, I see the same unshaven
fellow idling in a black limo
at our curb. He comes at midnight, craven,
lurking, stalking.   I step to the window
and say, *Listen, Death, I scorn your ego,*
your glib monotony, your repetition,
how everything you do is like an echo
of what you've always done. Where's your ambition,
Death?
        My mother's doing what she has never
done before: inventing her departure.

AT 10,000 FEET

While I arrow easily above a cloud up here,
the shadow of our airplane races through
a tiny neighborhood as if it were
an errand boy delivering dark news.

Help her. May they quickly find a cure,
I pray, all tense desire strapped to a seat
that's overdue to land: my mother's daughter,
scanning fragile roofs.
                              On a thread of street
I think I see her walking in her warmest
hat. It's not her, couldn't be. But I wonder
anyway, showering prayers down on—whoever—
as we fly into the darkness, hulking west,
shadows bulking in. Light wincing, slender,
gone.
        Into the faceless night, winging fast.

REUNION

Racing to get home, he guns his Jaguar
(*how could she be dying?*) down the highway.
A beauty, she was, elusive as the future,
his mother. Usually traveling on his birthday.

He couldn't fly. He needed to touch dirt
every inch of the way. To fly would be
to peel too fast the onion of his hurt.

She'd call. He wouldn't answer. He was busy.

Now it's ice he notices, gray molars
locked to dark bluffs, the way ice locks his heart
in steely winter logic.
                          But sun shimmers
on ice. The lock breaks. Love flows. Relief,
the melting! He steers toward his mother

knowing this fast trip might end in grief.

AFTER THE DEATH BED:
FOURTEEN LINES
SEPARATED AND WANDERING

Later that day they called and told us how.

Long since, he had memorized her song.

Don't ask me how we know the things we know.

And still the endless light refused to stop.

The things we see we can't be sure we see.

Lit by green fluorescence from the clock.

Already he knew just what she would say.

Time hacked the hours to minutes, tick tock.

There are long days we still look for a sign.

She closed her eyes. And then she closed her eyes.

Whatever he could do, he did it then.

What comes is later. And what goes is soon.

Not coincidentally, she sang.

And one more thing. The light this afternoon.

BURYING MY MOTHER

This is what our wandering life has come to.
Our dead stay where they're put, in different states.
We buried her beside the Texan, who
also loved her. Then we closed the gates.

None of us will join her. There's a spot
they dug for hours to slide my brother in.
He lies beside my father in her plot—
or what was hers once—beneath Nebraska sun.

In Philadelphia, now, I will not rave
or overstate my grief. I won't fly with flowers
to grace their level markers. I'm not brave.
Our family's scattered. Will be. Nothing's surer.

Who is she, elbow cocked against the sun,
waving to me this morning on the lawn?

GRIEF

And then it's like this: wood smoke blows
across the meadow and a woman is walking
with toast and coffee to a small round window,
where she watches pines raise their blackening
lattice-work against the silver fog.

Pine, she says. *Morning.*
                    Anything so she can
find a knob to steer the day. To stop the bog
from closing over that dear face again.

She is on duty, grieving. Waiting till when
she gets some further dispatch—she'll stay
where shadows swarm the landscape, where the fen
might swallow her, alive, as well.
                       Someday
she may return with news. Till then, for
now, let morning find itself without her.

HER CRY

that morning when she finds the tomb empty
leaps from her like the first bright geyser
sprung from the Titanic.
                              She bangs her knee
and ducks to look again. Her advisor,
John, warned her what a risk it was to come.

Holed up behind locked doors: the gang of guys
who claimed to love him. She runs her thumb
across the ledge where his dead body lies—

or rather doesn't. Her heart's a cypress;
she feels it forming a final growth-ring of grief:
his body gone, his lithe hand, the small scar
from a sharp chisel.
                              To what can she say yes?
Who is she now? Where to put belief?
Her cry gashes the fragile morning air.

PRAYING FOR THE DEAD

Do not go gentle into that good night.
—DYLAN THOMAS

I think of their last moments: a man in a boat
out there, rowing toward shore. The whoosh of quail.
A shot. And his retriever swimming out.

It's my father I've put on this lake in fall,
now that I know a thing or two, so I can spend
the kind of love on him that you could call
motherly. When his heart stutters, I send
this life preserver, dash this quick email-
of-a-prayer from this messy shore, my desk.

In fact, this is for all who've died. Take care
of them, eternal God: you know no time.
Bring calm to Jesus, wondering what to ask,
what he can let go, what he must keep,
before they bring the nails.
                              Hear this prayer:
Visit them with peace before they yield to sleep.

COMPLAINT: ONCE MORE ABOUT DEATH

Large doses [of rue] can cause violent
gastric pain, vomiting, systemic complications, and death.
—WIKIPEDIA, *under the entry "Ruta graveolens"*

More than I hate weeds, I hate the heaven of blue
blossoms that lap this meadow, looking milder
than water. This paradise murdered the ewe
I found on the trail, her carcass bewildered
by black flies.
     Why do you make us love
what kills us? And after grief, our failed
attempt to name the damage. *Goat's Rue.*
I write these words for a blaze on the trail.

Meanwhile you hide. No image, sign or word,
however shifting, can fix you—the Light
light changes to. I think of the bird
crashing against our window, dying to
unite with the reflected sun.
      Light kills.
Dazzling, unfathomable you are, and lethal.

THE VOICE

Be still and know that I am God.
—PSALM 46:10

Your terror, dear one, makes me love you,
lost from the others, there in the scary
blue meadow alone, where long before you,
your mothers talked to me. Human memory
is short. Surely you know that whatever
you build will fall from the shape you give it
back to dust. I am your creator.
Be calm as the oaks are calm. You flit
and dart in panic like a hummingbird.
Look, I'm here.
             You tell me I am silent.
In what tongue shall I speak? What words
would be clear? Try to curb your violent
questions. Why not believe the beauty you
see? I pour sun through oaks.
               What more do I have to do?

ROAD TO EMMAUS

After his funeral, all of the eleven
opted to find and mend their rotten nets,
to fish.
      What made them set—again—
the clock to three years earlier—before all bets
were off?
         God was dead. They fished as if
they'd never thought he'd crown them big shots
in the coming kingdom,
                 worked their skiffs
like crazy. Who can blame them? What shot
their nerves to pieces was the gory stare
of the reckless genius who'd left them pending
with nothing. Like fish gasping in the air.

Now frankly, their own stories needed ending.

He caught up to them at dusk. A maddening stranger
who told a cheerful story. What disaster?

WORKING TO SAVE YOURSELF

From here I can see her rowing on the lake,
or almost see her, riding house-high waves
that sweep her further out beyond the break—
—a dot—now gone, now there. As the water raves
and bucks, I row toward her, then God! upend
in savage wind, my boat flopping, fighting
itself and splitting. Waves thrash, my hands
slip off the boat. I call. The sky eats lightning.
I yell for help to save her.
                              She's me, but far
beyond the buoy in darkness.
                              I flick the light
on, sweep our dining room, taking such care,
my care might save her. I set her place, fold white
napkins into sailboats. They lean toward her.

Out there she feels them tow her back from danger.

THE LECTURE

You're stars! he tells us. *Every molecule*
in your fingers, bellies—long ago was cooking
at some star's core, then scattered out to cool.

What love I have flies to those atoms, looking
for years through empty interstellar weather
to find a soul and love it. The loneliness,
the bad odds.
          How strange we are: together
in this room by chance, this night, this once.

Then we resume our lives. The tall man
up front stabs his arm into his empty sleeve.

Not sure of what I am, I zip my coat,
stride out where lightning slices night. Sudden
thunder shakes the ground. A bellow heaves
from dark galactic space,
                 heaves from my own throat.

RUMMAGING THROUGH LANGUAGE TO FIND A SONNET

After her death, after the long black silence, after the sun rises, tips,
and spills pink between night-blackened pines, rosy fingers stroking
bare twigs of olive trees awake, dumb from sleet of winter and numb
embalming snows, after light spreads across the valley, creeping into crevices
of rocks, hesitating, as if to knock and ask permission, after the sun opens
its aperture to take in vineyards beneath my window the way light must have
explored air when God said *Let there be light* and dark cracked forever
like a geode divided by the strike of time,

when I see this precious, never-to-be-precisely-reiterated brightness,
I long to find some modest, sturdy cup, some strong bowl
of words to hold it: *Thursday.*
                              How lightness
drops from the womb of night like a white foal
this sudden morning, juddering to unbend,
breathing new air. Gathering herself to stand.

THE BUTTERFLY EFFECT

You could say the hurricane was stirred
when someone waved goodbye in China.
Heartbreak here can move the ocean there.
A scarlet bloom in England can define a
bloodshot sunset in Japan.
                          Some days when
I make my last turn beside our maple I'm aware
I'm safe, I'm home: I'm grateful. And then
a woman in Hawaii shuts her door.

Yesterday I had a root canal.
Who cares? But suppose the doctor sank
his bit straight through my feet, the floor, the soil,
earth's core, and up.
                        Imagine the drill
making its point to sleepy Buddhist monks
as it split the calm of their reflecting pool.

WHAT WAS I THINKING?

Not of the fawn, but his terror, leaping through shade,
crimson flower blooming in his side,
and how he fell.
                  Not the lily; its long fade
and droop.
            Not Sally, but the way she died.

This was the land of shadow I passed through,
hearing behind me death's rasping, wintery
breath. As he stalked me, how tired I grew,
how sick of grief. How I laughed bitterly.

Then how capably one sudden day
radiant health returned: the fawn, the lily.
Sally's now tranquil spirit.
                My new naivete
wonders at sunlight, songs, the raging sea,
even my hands: I spread them. Nails and hinges,
the knuckles like little mountain ranges.

REVERSAL

The eggs, broken, scrambled, fried and fragrant
on a plate, slip back into their shells;
each smooth white egg sails toward its vagrant
mother chicken, roosts in a fertile cell.

The melody beats back to eighth notes
which settle, dark spots on the snowy staff
of bass and treble clefs, then briefly float
through Bach's wine-stained shirt into his laugh.

The house remembers when it was imagined.
The nails and bolts that hold the walls in place
fly back to hardware bins. The rafters, stunned,
revert to drawings and desire.
                              So geese,
who honked across this troubled sky last fall,
welcome back. This chance to undo it all.

NOTES TO YOURSELF

Remember how you stumbled on that fence,
gashing your knee? Your precious blood seeped
out, the breakers hissed *impermanence!*
The ocean frowned before you fell asleep
under the sun's fierce glare. Wind stirred
and sand stretched, tranquil, to the edge of sky.

You must guard your childhood now; you're your
own mother here today on the sandy rise
beside sea oats.
                    At noon put down your book,
pick up that child, carry her from too much sun,
indoors.
            Remember how your mother took
you gently up, then folded up the ocean,
tucked it safely under her arm, swept
the beach into a jar?
                        How long it's kept. It's kept.

IV

Silence is the only phenomenon today that is "useless."
It does not fit into the world of profit and utility:
it simply is. It seems to have no other purpose;
it cannot be exploited. . . . It cannot be replaced by
anything else; it cannot be exchanged with anything else.
There is nothing behind it to which it can be related
except the Creator Himself.

—MAX PICARD,
The World of Silence

AT THE OCEAN

No shopping mall. No book. No carnival,
no binoculars, or other nifty gadgets
to elaborate upon the waves, which fill
this whole frame with their fidget, fidget
fidget. Thrashed by unrelenting breeze,
the green-gray water curls and fizzes.
The noise of a great body, hauling its wheeze
and hiss, endless, blank, with no *because*
or purpose.

        Therefore the mind finds metaphor.
Beyond the breakers, ancient women wash
their bed sheets, splashing white suds against the fire
of sunset, tumbling laundry till I feel the slosh,
could name their names.

            How I see better what
is there

      after sitting quietly with what is not.

THE PROBLEM WITH SILENCE

Last week I was restless as the ocean.
I paced the winter beach in sleet, alone
when I didn't want to be alone. My phone,
silent. I longed to talk, to hear some human
voice.
       I called: *Let me know you're here.*
You didn't answer.
                Then I knew how poor
I was. I picked up conch shells, hoping to decipher
their loopy shapes. I tried to read blank air.
I was nothing but flayed hunger, my need
more raw than the roiling sea or freezing rain.

Back in the city, I'm going mad with speed
and noise. My heart's inflamed with neon.
Now I wish I could be poor again.

PHILADELPHIA: WALKING TO WORK ON THE FIRST DAY OF SPRING

Bright sun. The breeze on my arms. On his leash
a white poodle strolling like a plume
of breath in winter, leading his person: their swish,
such class.
            Oh, finally to get out! The bloom,
the yes of my re-waking body.
                        Until the bus
burps smoke. And far above, a wrecking ball
bangs a storefront open like a dollhouse,
its tremors traveling up my spine.
                      Hell!
a guy yells, weaving between the bleat
of outraged car horns
                  and suddenly I'm filling
up with blare and clamor.
                Then across the street
I see her, walking, silent, alert, willing
herself to be here, smiling.
               I watch her pass, quiet
shining from her face and quiet rising from her habit.

SILENCE

is what, I think, I long for.
                              Rain slams its
fists against the leaves. A wood thrush flutes
his signature and then again, persists.
Deep rumbles as a tree upends, its twisted roots
exposed.
              There may be no such thing
as silence. When John Cage tried to cage it,
his clean 4-plus minutes seethed with the circling
of his blood: his own heart sent its
lub*dub* lub*dub* around the concert hall.

But still I long for stillness, white and vast
as an Alp glistening in the sun, its tall
massive shoulders shawled with light. One last
finch flying—one mute speck on snow.

How wanting stillness still might make it so.

RUAH

Write me a sonnet with the wind in it, please.

—for my student, Jeremy

Because we both heard the whine and bark
of the hungry storm last night—he there, me here—
the wind tossing itself through the dark
between us, he wrote and asked.

                              So, *Wind, appear,*
I say, because he wants it. Flap and nip
and yowl, Chinook, Simoom, Diablo,
Today the sizzling breeze, the deadly flip
to freezing squalls tomorrow.

                              As breath blows
through flutes, blow through these words, let us draw
you in and out, be near, be quiet, be night
and morning, be nothing but the bright *ah!*
you are.

              I am the window where you write,
I am the breeze you see through it, the bird
ruffling in the wind. I am the first and the last word.

THE SOUL LONGS FOR HOME

When what I have right here
                                    is what I want
why is it then
                    I miss it most?
When our old birch turns yellow in the gaunt
fall, I long for the way its leaves can cast
down their gold to make the dull grass glint,
as if the tree were mirrored by the ground.

The present's all we know, but I'm not present
hard or true enough, maybe not kind
enough to grasp it.
                    I hear the house finch,
moving west, wing-thrash. Flash. Gone.

Even when I'm home, why can't I quench
the city I take everywhere with me? Even
here in Philadelphia, as the white
moon slips down the skyline, I long for it.

STUDY: HOW THE LEAF FALLS

And then a squall tumbles it toward heaven
and spins it in a whiff of dying grass,
not far, but farther than it's ever gone
from the old birch. It's yellow and has mass
that it can feel, now, since it let go.
It falls, allows itself to spin, then rocks
in the hammock of a breeze and so below
it settles, gold on the ground-bed.
                                    The tricks,
the joy, how she budded, stiffened
like a green sail in the insistent wind
and held. How she waved goodbye like a hand.
How, together, they transformed sound
itself, the sister leaves. Gentle pizzazz
of memory, rustling, swishing, all that jazz.

EVERYWHERE YOU LOOK YOU SEE LILACS

and better yet,
                  just blossoming in woozy
pink and white, smell the peonies
that will cast off their clothes like floozies
soon. Ponder the indolent fat bees
like tiny blimps that hover over them,
perfectly content with where they are
this morning. Nothing's missing in the flame
of this slow day. Sun through Douglas fir
cascading now, the earth complete and here:
once, currently, forever. How not traveling,
we've still traveled everywhere. How far
it's possible to go without unraveling
maps or charts. To get there with no drive,
no fear, not even any hunger to arrive.

ATTEMPT

Be present with your want of a Deity
and you shall be present with the Deity.

—Thomas Traherne

Sometimes I lose you, as if you were a stallion
and the barn door's left ajar. Or I'm due someplace
and can't remember where. In my hellion
hair and ripped work shirt, I ransack the place
to find my datebook. Gone. Or I've dropped
my glasses and I'm crawling on all fours
to swab the floor with outstretched hands. I mop
blindly, my heart stuttering with fear.
Don't tell me you're not a stallion. I know.
You're not some destination. But I want to
tell you what it's like to search, although
the words are clumsy. Vapor.

                      What it comes to:
You are the sky, the boat, the oars, the water.
You are the soul that longs to row and you're the rower.

BORDER CROSSING

—for Steve Shoemaker

Mid-September. The cicada's ardent song
grows deafening. Wind rubs the oak's old joints.
Something's going to happen. The sky goes wrong,
purples.

       And I'm back at the checkpoint,
the guard with his gun pawing through my luggage.
My heart skipping its ragged rope—child
that I became—as he harangued in a language
I didn't understand,

            then grinned and piled
my stuff into his bag, and waved me through
without it.

       That's the kind of line we're about
to cross. You will lay down your precious words,
your name. They won't be any use. You'll
climb the highest pass, wordless, hear a shout,
a greeting and

          the sky's all sudden golden birds.

THE HAUNTING

We'll build in sonnets pretty rooms.

—John Donne

Why do we love what's miniature
and take it to our hearts? The yellow walls
as small as stamps, the furniture
and rugs no bigger than a toddler's thumbnail.
A working fireplace the size of a box
for commas. A Cheerio wreath. Tiny kindling
to feed the fire in case it's flummoxed
by the teeny breeze.
                              All this dwindling
makes me uneasy. I step back to gauge
its spooky cuteness. Nothing, even the fire
spitting its shiny wrath can leave this page.
Though no one's home, the chandelier
sways mutely. A white snowfall of numb
silence waits outside each little room.

NIGHTMARE

The book is dead. John Donne's not humming
and dashing down the stairs. He never was.
No *Moby Dick,* no late light gleaming
in a reader's window.

     No reader, because
words are only letters, dumb, drifting down
like brown leaves on the lawn. So erase
the poems I've written here.

      Young Beethoven
is gone. Rembrandt's gone. In their place
cold iambs.

     And then I turn to see a finch crying
at the bird feeder in his red bib: *bird,*
bird, bird, and all around him, flying
maples, clouds vying and merging—the word
Sophie, laughing under the wind chime
as she writes the perfect letters of her name.

THE COBBLER

You ring his bell. He climbs from the basement,
where he shapes shoes in silence. Hasn't spoken
a word all morning.

              Now: *They need replacement
heels, new soles.* You bow together over broken
boots. You're embarrassed at how homely,
how foul they've grown. You almost feel despair.
He listens, strokes them:

                     No, they might be holy.
He brushes away the dust. Your eyes blur
with his love of boots.

              The earth is dust, we're all
dust. He picks up his shoemaker's hammer
and gently taps the sole. Above his bench, his awls,
his busy knives and scissors, this reminder:

    Pilgrim, there is no path.
                Attend.
                  *You're breaking
unmarked ground. You find the path by walking.*

SHOES

The soil is bare now, nor can foot feel, being shod.
—GERARD MANLEY HOPKINS

Some are hardly more than a rubber stutter
against a foot. The slap of flip-flops
for instance, so sweet and sharp. The utter
honesty of sandals. Red sneakers. But what stops
the opera of shoes point blank is the libretto
scripted just to showcase silk and rhinestone,
which ride into the room on high stilettos
stacked from cowhide, molded of snakeskin
and dyed puce.
           Once there was a garden
where finches flew like graceful, half-formed thought
above the rippling grasses. Hooves of fleet
deer grazed thyme. No one needed pardon
for stealing skin from calves. No one sought
style.
      Imagine how new grass felt on their feet.

FAREWELL

The last heel's cobbled.

We check his empty rooms, close the door.
Finches flash by, nest empty, summer gleam
of yellow gone. Everything we long for,
we make ours through longing. Apples seem
crisper, sweeter when they're conjured
than if I taste them on my tongue. May we find
ourselves by letting ourselves go. May absence cure
our craving. May sweet silence not confound
us. Goodbye, good path, good rooms, good shoes,
good walking.
               Dusk falls. So much goes on
that we can't grasp. Trees hush, the vast
dimmer switch of sun dials down and noise
relents.
               Our shoes are worn. The cobbler's gone.
And in his empty shop stands the last last.

ACKNOWLEDGMENTS

I did not write these sonnets alone, but in the company of friends, the poets Deborah Burnham, Devon Miller-Duggan, and Elaine Terranova, who have faithfully read and commented on them. I am grateful for both the pleasure of their company and their wise counsel. Thanks also to my husband, E. Daniel Larkin III, who has written at least one fine sonnet himself, and has supported this project from day one.

I'm equally grateful to the journal editors who had faith in these poems, often before they had reached their final form. Special thanks to Mark S. Burrows, who accepted some of these poems as Poetry Editor at several journals and then wrote me to suggest that we work together to gather the sonnets into a book. The following journals published earlier versions of poems in this manuscript, sometimes under different titles or in earlier drafts.

Anglican Theological Review: "So You're Losing Your Memory?"
Arts: "The Longing Sonnet"
BigCityLit: "Notes to Yourself"
Blackbird: "Grief"
The Christian Century: "After the Butterfly Completes the First Leg of her Thousand Mile Migration," "Burying My Mother," "Her Cry," "Poinsettia," "Reunion," "Self Examination," "Farewell," "The Cobbler Goes Out of Business," "Badlands"

Christianity and Literature: "The Knock on Your Door
  Disguised as a Sonnet"

The Cresset: "About the Butterfly Effect," "Baker,"
  "The Cobbler," "Praying for the Dead"

The Cumberland Review: "Border Crossing"

Dappled Things: "Ruah," "Shoes"

First Things: "Road to Emmaus"

The Georgia Review: "Learning to See"

Hudson Review: "The Lecture," "Silence," "Mendelssohn
  Finds the St. Matthew Passion," "At the Ocean," "Study:
  How the Leaf Falls"

Image: "In the Beginning," "The Music Before the Music,"
  "Reversal"

Inisfree: "Everywhere You Look You See Lilacs," "Song of the
  Street," "Rock," "Philadelphia: Walking to Work on the
  First Day of Spring," "Rummaging through Language to
  Find a Sonnet"

Literature and Belief: "Foreboding"

Measure: "To the Cardinal Watching Me Shower"

Relief: "Rembrandt: Late Self-Portrait," "Sophie Learns to
  Print *Sophia,*" "While Hiking Back to the House without
  Pen and Paper, I Make Mental Notes"

Shenandoah: "Finch"

Sojourners: "Breaking the Blue Bowl"

Solo Café: "Summer Camp"

Spiritus: "Attempt"

The Southern Review: "The Creation," "The Haunting"

Vineyards: "The Problem with Silence," "The Violinist"

ABOUT PARACLETE PRESS

Who We Are

As the publishing arm of the Community of Jesus, Paraclete Press presents a full expression of Christian belief and practice—from Catholic to Evangelical, from Protestant to Orthodox, reflecting the ecumenical charism of the Community and its dedication to sacred music, the fine arts, and the written word. We publish books, recordings, sheet music, and video/DVDs that nourish the vibrant life of the church and its people.

What We Are Doing

BOOKS | PARACLETE PRESS BOOKS show the richness and depth of what it means to be Christian. While Benedictine spirituality is at the heart of who we are and all that we do, our books reflect the Christian experience across many cultures, time periods, and houses of worship.

We have many series, including *Paraclete Essentials*; *Paraclete Fiction*; *Paraclete Poetry*; *Paraclete Giants*; and for children and adults, *All God's Creatures*, books about animals and faith; and *San Damiano Books*, focusing on Franciscan spirituality. Others include *Voices from the Monastery* (men and women monastics writing about living a spiritual life today), *Active Prayer*, and new for young readers: *The Pope's Cat*. We also specialize in gift books for children on the occasions of Baptism and First Communion, as well as other important times in a child's life, and books that bring creativity and liveliness to any adult spiritual life.

The MOUNT TABOR BOOKS series focuses on the arts and literature as well as liturgical worship and spirituality; it was created in conjunction with the Mount Tabor Ecumenical Centre for Art and Spirituality in Barga, Italy.

MUSIC | The PARACLETE RECORDINGS label represents the internationally acclaimed choir *Gloriæ Dei Cantores*, the *Gloriæ Dei Cantores Schola*, and the other instrumental artists of the *Arts Empowering Life Foundation*.

Paraclete Press is the exclusive North American distributor for the Gregorian chant recordings from St. Peter's Abbey in Solesmes, France. Paraclete also carries all of the Solesmes chant publications for Mass and the Divine Office, as well as their academic research publications.

In addition, PARACLETE PRESS SHEET MUSIC publishes the work of today's finest composers of sacred choral music, annually reviewing over 1,000 works and releasing between 40 and 60 works for both choir and organ.

VIDEO | Our video/DVDs offer spiritual help, healing, and biblical guidance for a broad range of life issues including grief and loss, marriage, forgiveness, facing death, understanding suicide, bullying, addictions, Alzheimer's, and Christian formation.

Learn more about us at our website:
www.paracletepress.com
or phone us toll-free at 1.800.451.5006

SCAN
TO
READ
MORE

You may also be interested in . . .

UNQUIET VIGIL
Paul Quenon, ocso

ISBN 978-1-61261-560-8 | $19.99 | Trade paper

"The poems of *Unquiet Vigil* rise out of a more intense experience of reality, evoke aspects of that reality not universally acknowledged, and re-express them in exquisite and economical language."
—Michael Casey, ocso

EYES HAVE I THAT SEE
John Julian, ojn

ISBN 978-1-61261-640-7 | $18 | Trade paper

"A rich distillation of word and craft born over thirty years of the author doing the deep, hard work of sinking into silence."
—*Anglican Theological Review*

CHARLES OF THE DESERT
A Life in Verse
William Woolfitt

ISBN 978-1-61261-764-0 | $20 |Trade paper

"These poems—lush, accomplished lyrics gathered by a delicate narrative thread—present a profound and savory confusion. Spoken in the in the voice of the book's titular persona, Charles de Foucauld, the poems present genuine exultation, vertiginous truth."
—Scott Cairns

Available at bookstores
Paraclete Press 1-800-451-5006
www.paracletepress.com